Why Not

Try God?

BY THE AUTHOR OF

"My Rendezvous with Life"

Why Not Try God?

By
Mary Pickford

Afterword by
Dr. Anke Brouwers

NORTHERN ROAD
CULVER CITY, CALIFORNIA

2013

Edition editor, Andi Hicks
Series editor, Hugh Munro Neely

Published by
Northern Road Productions
P.O. Box 954
Culver City, California 90232-0954

find us at: northern-road.com
Cover design by Hugh Munro Neely
Book design by Andi Hicks

IF you had a million dollars in the bank but didn't know how to write a check, it wouldn't do you much good, would it?

If you had a car in your garage but had lost the key with which to start it, you wouldn't get anywhere very fast, would you?

That's about the way humanity is operating today.

Quite a few years ago, when I was unhappy and greatly troubled, I found out how I could call upon a power that, if I used the right key, would always give me everything I needed.

Today I know more than ever that there is a beneficent power available to me which will always comfort me and guide me and allow me to be happy, even amid troubles and heartbreaks.

I found out about the power of right thinking. And my discovery has brought me so much joy and given me so much spiritual light in the hardest hours of my life that I want to share it with all who care to try it.

Of course I have always thought it was well to be cheerful if you possibly could, to be brave in the face of disaster, and to smile instead of cry when hurt. That was just a sort of Pollyanna philosophy, and it was pretty good in fair weather. And I spent a great deal of time waiting for the day when everything would be just right and I could always be lighthearted and contented.

But I didn't know then what I found out later: that right thinking is a power, the power with which you tune into God, and that it can actually change conditions of every kind, no matter how serious and complicated they may seem to be. They may not be changed in exactly the way we plan, but they will be changed in the way that will be best for us, best for everybody concerned. And with this right thinking

2

there comes from the same divine source the wisdom and ability to maintain our poise and happiness under all circumstances, and the courage to look ahead with expectancy of good.

The other day a young girl came to see me.

She said, "Mary, I'm licked. I'm in a lot of trouble and I can't see any way out. You have some sort of system that keeps you happy even when outward things are wrong. Would it help me? I'm desperate!"

I told her it would help anyone who would try it.

And then she said, rather doubtfully, "You know, I'm not religious, Mary. I don't really believe in God."

I said, "I wasn't religious, either. And I used to hate what I thought God was."

Then I told her about a time when I was quite a little girl and my mother found me sitting under a lamp post, talking heatedly to myself.

"What are you doing, darling?" she called casually.

"I'm hating God," I said emphatically.

Well, of course, my mother, who was a devout Christian, was horrified. But even she couldn't alter my youthful opinion that God was a pretty mean old fellow. Mean and spiteful. He would, I had been informed, be very angry if He found out that I loved my mother better than I did Him. He would also punish me for a number of things which didn't seem to me very important. More than that, it was my firm conviction that He treated lots of good people very badly. One of my little playmates died suddenly, bringing bitter grief and sorrow to her devoted mother, her brothers and sisters and the entire neighborhood. People told me that, "it was God's will."

I rebelled. I made up my mind that as far as I was concerned I wouldn't be a hypocrite and pretend to love such a God. I didn't want anything to do with Him. I didn't like the way He did things.

Lots of people still feel that way, I imagine, especially young people.

But since then many things have happened in my experience. I have known great happiness. I have known equally great unhappiness. Most of the material things that people daydream about I have had in abundance. But success and fame, wealth and innumerable good friends all over the world can be of little help at a time when trouble strikes into the affections, or sorrow and worry and despair sweep over one like a wet, black fog, obscuring everything.

How true it is that what looks like the end of the road in our personal experience, is only the turn in the road, the beginning of a new and more beautiful journey.

It was at one of these road turns, and it looked like a tragic one too, that I made a discovery of great importance to myself — I was carrying around with me a concept of God that was, to say the least, ridiculous. So I discarded it.

That was the first step. The next was to try and find out for myself just what God really was like and how and in what way I was related to Him. And that was the beginning of a glorious adventure.

Hunting for truth. Hunting for it in myself, in my work, in those I came in contact with, in everything.

And God ceased to be a formidable, threatening deity up in the skies. Instead, as I explored mentally, He came to be an all-wise, loving, friendly presence, filling all space everywhere and closer to me than the very air I breathed. Then I began looking for the God element in people, in circumstances and in events; and the more I looked, the more I found and, correspondingly, the greater happiness I experienced.

God became, not only my Big Boss, but my unseen Good Companion, my Silent Partner, my Counselor. He was always by my side. It became increasingly clear that creation was the work of but one Mind, or intelligence, and that this Mind belonged to you and to me and to every one, governing us all with perfect understanding and in perfect harmony.

This may seem extremely doubtful to someone who, at the moment, may be encountering great trials and tribulations.

But let me relate this. A California teacher was explaining to a group of boys that Good, or God, was everywhere. One of them asked, "Well, is he in the jails and prisons?" Before she could get an answer ready another boy said, "God is in them but those guys don't know it." And that's just what I had to find out for myself — that God really was around everywhere but I didn't know it.

All the Good that there is can be ours right now if we but tune in with God.

And the only instrument with which we can tune in is our own thinking. But we can't get any more good out of the power of God unless we do tune in than we can get out of electricity if we don't turn on the switch.

If Edison had never set up his laboratory the electric light would be there just the same. If Marconi had never lived, a wireless would still be possible. If there had been no Alexander Graham Bell, the principles that make our telephones would exist just the same. But we wouldn't be able to use them because we wouldn't know how. Now I believe, and in a relative degree have been able to prove, that God is a great power, which we can use whenever and wherever we choose, by our own right thinking. Certainly we have nothing to lose by just trying it. Sometimes we may fail. We may even do a lot of failing. But that is because we haven't learned yet how to work it perfectly. But we will succeed often enough to make us want to go on and on and, in time, become perfect operators.

The great electrical genius, Charles Steinmetz, was once asked by Roger Babson, the business statistician, what line of research would see the greatest development in the next fifty years. Instead of mentioning some line of electrical application, as one would have thought, he said he believed the greatest discovery would be made along spiritual lines.

"Here is a force," he said, "which history clearly teaches has been the greatest power in the development of men and history. Yet we have merely been playing with it and have never seriously studied it as we have the physical forces. Some day people will learn that material things do not bring happiness and are of little use in making men and women creative and powerful. Then the scientists of the world will turn their laboratories over to the study of God and prayer and the spiritual forces, which as yet have hardly been touched. When this day comes the world will see more advancement in one generation than it has in the past four."

Why shouldn't we be that generation? Why shouldn't that time be now?

For too long a time we have been trying the other way. We have followed the jungle method of the survival of the fittest — fighting, struggling, ruthless and cruel! Result? Look around you — despair, confusion, dishonesty, failure, economic wreckage and almost utter collapse under trials.

Nearly all of us are beset by trials and tribulations.

Why not not try God?

The life of each one of us is a continual process of thought. That's all there is to us anyway. When we think, we experience; when we don't think, we "just ain't." Thought is the most vital and powerful thing in the entire universe. All the good and evil in the world is the result of right or wrong thinking and each of us is contributing something to the sum total one way or the other every second.

When our thinking is clear enough we become a transparency for God, or the Mind of the universe, to shine through. Then we experience good results and we have real and lasting prosperity, success, happiness and health. But when we are not tuned in the troubles come to us.

A very wise man once said, "We see only our own thoughts and in some way or other they become externalized as our environment and experience, and so the world we seem to be experiencing *without*, is really the world we are seeing *within*. How could we possibly think one way and have experiences in the opposite direction?"

Isn't it wonderful to realize that no one in the whole world, no government, no bank, no other person, no anything, can interfere with what each of us chooses to think! Like a radio, each one of us may tune in the good and instantly shut off the bad, or let in the bad and switch off the good.

Nothing in the world can make you conscious of failure or unhappiness unless you think about it. Nothing in all the world can harm you without your individual consent. Whatever we hold in thought automatically becomes real to us — externalizes itself in experience.

A very remarkable woman whom I know recently lost her husband. They had been very much in love and extremely happy. When I saw her some weeks later she radiated a tranquility and confidence which was inspiring. I asked her how she had achieved it. She said, "All the water in the world cannot sink a ship unless it gets *inside* the ship. All the sorrow in the world cannot sink a person unless it gets *inside* the mind. I have kept my mind so full of good thoughts, so full of thoughts for others, that there hasn't been any room for sorrow and self-pity to get in."

I have been glad many times since then that she told me, because I have found that it works. Unlike most women, I have never been able to work out my intimate problems in private. I have to do it in front of the whole world, for the world knows what is happening to me professionally, domestically and personally almost as soon as I do myself. And so, in a way, I become at times more or less of a target for flying rumors and counter-rumors, hasty judgments and thoughtless gossip.

But I've learned not to let it leak in. And the more difficult the problem the harder I try to find the God-element, or the good-element, in people and things, and the more I try to think about others as I would have them think about me.

Some years ago when Mr. Fairbanks and I were in China we were the guests of a delightful couple, a professor of archeology and his wife. One evening during dinner the husband spoke of taking us the next morning to see a famous gateway, one of the oldest and most beautiful things in China. And his wife said, "Oh, don't take Mrs. Fairbanks there! The gateway is beautiful but I never can see it because of the filthy, dirty people that are always gathered there."

Each of them had their choice. He saw the great beauty and artistry of the gateway. She saw the ugliness and dirt of the human beings beneath it.

There is a great deal in life that is fine and beautiful which we refuse to see. We keep our eyes glued on the dangers, the difficulties, the unpleasant things. We soak ourselves in them. They finally occupy our thoughts and these thoughts are manifested in human experience.

"As a man thinketh in his heart, so is he."

That is what you will find and *prove* if you will just try it. Of course you have heard it many times. Perhaps you thought it was only a nice sounding sentiment. Do you realize that it means that whatever is happening to you or to me at this very minute is absolutely the result of what each of us has been putting into our minds, what each of us has been thinking for years? And do you realize that what will happen tomorrow will be the result, in a great degree, of what you are thinking today? You and I cannot possibly escape the result of our thoughts.

So our concern is not really with external things at all, these being secondary, but with our thoughts.

Let's go into the laboratory of our minds and see about all this.

The first thing you find is — *I am.*

All right. How do you know you *are?*

Because you can think about it. The moment you can't think about it you have no consciousness of existence and so, you just are not. Then what is the primary fact of existence? Why, thought, of course. The power of thinking. Take that away and man is nothing. Your mind knows that you are and that makes you.

Your thinking is the medium through which everything comes to you.

Then, thought is the most vital and essential thing about man; that which connects each of us with this wonderful, precious gift of life.

Then oughtn't *thinking* to come first? Oughtn't it to be *the* power? Doesn't it seem rather silly to believe that this great force, this one necessary force, is just something that can be ruled by the body, by conditions, and by outside beliefs, and that we can't individually do anything about it?

We've put the cart before the horse, not only in this, but in most of our theories of existence. Thought is the great power of the universe — not body, nor matter, nor conditions.

So right where you are at this very minute, no matter how black and difficult your situation, you have one priceless possession. You can think. And if you have thought your way into any kind of trouble, and that is the only way we get into trouble, you can turn at any time you choose and think your way out again. Nothing can hold you there but your thinking. Nothing can free you but your thinking. You are the dictator of your own world of thinking. And what you think, and only what you think, goes. We set our own boundaries and limits. We alone set the margins around our thinking and our experience.

How little we know of the marvelous universe unfolding all about us! Sir James Jeans, the great scientist, who has told us such astonishing things about astronomy, said, not so long ago, that our universe seemed to be nearer a great thought than to a great machine. When he was asked if this meant that the universe is one of thought, he is quoted as saying, "I would say as a speculation, not as a scientific fact, that the universe and all material objects in it — atoms, stars and nebulae — are merely creations of thought — of course, not of your individual mind or mine, but of some great universal Mind underlying and coordinating all our minds. The most we can say is that scientific knowledge seems to be moving in this direction." And at another time he said, "It may be, it seems to me, that each individual consciousness is a brain cell in a universal mind."

Isn't that fascinating? Each of us part of a vast, cosmic intelligence? Each of us necessary in his place, no matter where that may be, for the eternal Mind to function through?

Scientists have now analyzed matter into some kind of atom, which is supposed to be composed chiefly of ether. There they are temporarily held up. What forms that ether into us — and into this great, orderly, beautiful, magnificent, and incredible universe in which we live? What holds the stars in their courses and brings the oak from the acorn and the sun up over the horizon every morning?

It is possible to choose to think anything you like. But the best choice is to believe that it is God, a universal Mind, a creative, benevolent intelligence.

Now what connects us with God? Our thoughts. What gives us the use of that great power which has put upon this planet all that every one of us needs forever? Our thinking.

God is a twenty-four-hour station. All you need to do is to plug in. You plug in with your thinking. Truthful thinking. Good thinking. Kind thinking. Unselfish thinking. And then you can have and use all the Love, all the Power, all the Courage, all the Energy, all the Cheerfulness, all the Activity and all the Kindliness of God.

A little boy I know, who wasn't the least bit religious in an orthodox way, but who had an intense interest in God, had some trouble with his ear. The doctor said that the ear was in bad shape and would have to be operated on. The youngster said nothing then, but when the subject came up later he calmly remarked that he wouldn't need any operation. "Mama," he said, "God made my ear. It must have been quite a job, and if He could do it in the first place it would be awfully funny if He couldn't attend to its upkeep." When the doctor called the next time the ear was well.

And *wouldn't* it be awfully funny, when you stop to think about it, if the power which fashioned us, which brought us into being, and which needs us to function through, couldn't attend to our upkeep?

But we must make our contact; we must tune in; we must be receptive. We should never be afraid to claim for ourselves everything we need. It is our privilege to have all good today. We don't need to postpone it. Why wait for heaven when we can have it here. Heaven is within — it is within our thinking.

If we are irritated, doubtful, fearful, angry, resentful or worried, we are expecting evil. We have opened the door for it and that's what we will get. That formula will bring its inevitable result.

If we are happy, courageous, cheerful, unselfish and sure of our rights as God's children, that formula will have its results too. Faith is the expectancy of good. Fear is the expectancy of evil.

Well, who's doing the expecting? What you expect, you invite into your mind; what you permit to remain in your mind has to externalize itself, which it will do in some way, and at some time in your experience. All history proves this. So why not start now expecting good, expecting health, expecting plenty, expecting happiness? Because you are; you can.

But when you set up that laboratory in your mind where you are going to produce right thinking and make your high voltage contact with the creative energy of the cosmos — which men call God — you will have a couple of visitors right away.

I call them Madame Flitmajigger and Professor Poofinfoos.

Madame Flitmajigger looks a little bit like the Duchess in *Alice in Wonderland* and she just can't bear to see anybody happy. She's always sticking her nose in other people's business. The moment she hears of anyone planning something nice, or feeling unusually well or happy, in she bounces with some observation that puts clouds all over one's blue sky. She's the one who says "Aren't you feeling well today? You don't look very well." And, "Why did you buy *that* hat? It's very unbecoming." And, "You really ought to know what she is saying about you — gabble, gabble, gabble — and between you and me and don't say that I said it — gabble, gabble, gabble!" Flitmajigger is just an old meanie.

Then, when she gets you upset and unhappy, along comes old Professor Poofinfoos, the granddaddy of all the liars. I invented him myself. He is my symbol of the devil, of personified evil. I found that I was making altogether too much of what we call the problem of evil. It seemed to me that evil was chiefly ignorance and an inability to see and comprehend good.

In the Bible I learned that the devil was only a liar and really had no importance or influence at all except with those who wanted to be an audience for him. History, I felt, had made the devil far too imposing and consequential. If I had any at all I wanted him to be ridiculous and so old Professor Poofinfoos came into being.

He's almost too silly to be described, but I'll try to tell you what he's like. To call him a half-wit would be almost too complimentary. His head goes up into a point, on top of which are three feathers for no good reason at all. He has no brain space. His nose is large and drooping. It has been knocked out of shape by too much pressure into other people's affairs. He has mean little eyes, which see only discordant things, and, having no character, he has a terrible-looking chin.

He has a turned-down, liar's mouth and peculiar ears, which turn in all directions, enabling him to listen to all the trouble that may be around. His torso is shaped like a pear and overly inflated with hot air about people. He has skinny legs, unpleasant looking skinny legs, and his clumsy feet with the upturned toes are real "bog trotters." He has a tail. All devils have to have tails. But the professor's is a sad-looking one, twisted, and broken in a number of places where alert thinkers have slammed the door on him.

Poofinfoos is always hanging around at our mental doors trying to get inside and tell us a lie about somebody or something. He wants us to believe that God did not make a perfect world, that He isn't capable of managing it and taking care of you and me, and that everything is just saturated with misfortune and calamity.

The moment we wake up, the professor will be lurking close by waiting for a chance to tell us how badly we feel and what an unfortunate day we have ahead of us. Start downtown and he's apt to roost on your shoulder and begin a whispering campaign to convince you that you are not as capable as you used to be and never, really, were much good. If you listen to him, if you believe his suggestions about your present and future limited prospects and the "awfulness" of your mistakes in the past, he'll not only sink you into the deepest depression, but he may destroy your usefulness to yourself, to your loved ones and to humanity.

He's a dreadful liar. He's tricky. But he's a big bluff.

He'll tell you that you are broke and that you can't do anything about it because there is a depression. He'll tell you that you are sick and that when you are sick you just have to be sick, that's all. He'll tell you again and again that you are too old, too young, too limited, too inexperienced, too handicapped and too this and too that. If he convinces you, if you accept what he says as true, he's hooked you.

But you don't have to be hooked. The next time any kind of trouble comes to you, instead of accepting it immediately as a fact and bemoaning your fate, treat it as a suggestion from old Professor Poofinfoos, trying to unload something on you contrary to your happiness and best interests. And watch the results. You will be astonished. Your arguments with him will amuse you and make you laugh, and as you laugh your problems will start shrinking and sooner or later they will disappear. For remember, Poofinfoos is only a big liar. He isn't true at all; and all the things he has been telling you are lies.

As you look back through history you will observe that all the men and women who accomplished really worth-while results did so because they never had anything to do with Poofinfoos. They wouldn't listen to him. They did the thinking and the talking and not the professor.

When Poofinfoos told Columbus that he couldn't find a new world and that he was crazy, Columbus yawned in his face and ignored him.

If Abraham Lincoln had listened to him and accepted his suggestions of defeat and failure, the world would never have heard of him.

And so it is throughout history.

Poofinfoos wants every one to be miserable. He never wants anyone to succeed. But there is only one door through which he can reach any of us and that is the door of our own consent.

You are a king and you rule over your own life. You rule your human experience with your own thoughts. In other words, you make your own world of thought; you preside with dictatorial power over your own private world of consciousness. And you rule ably or badly according to the quality of the thinking that you alone permit to go on.

The only way that mind can move is through thought — through your thought.

And the Mind which created everything, which guides everything and which sustains everything, will move for you, work for you, bring your purposes to pass and your prayers to fulfillment, if you will but do your part.

Today is a new day. You will get out of it just what you put into it.

However, if you have made mistakes, even serious mistakes, there is always another chance for you. And supposing you have tried and failed again and again, you may have a fresh start any moment you choose, for this thing that we call "failure" is not the falling down, but the staying down. And we can always take courage in the fact that we are part of the universe, God's universe, and not victims of it.

Most of us want to live in a world of goodness, of love, of friendliness, of happiness, of contentment, of abundance, of success, of joy and of harmonious relationships, and more and more I am coming to see that if we would experience these things, each of us must first of all plant them in our individual worlds of thought. For, "whatsoever a man soweth, that shall he also reap."

The kingdom of God is — where? Up in the clouds? Over on the other side of the mountain? Beyond the experience called death? Not at all. "The kingdom of God is *within you*." Could anything he plainer than that?

The biggest thrill you will ever get will be when you see that you have accomplished a great purpose through right thinking.

"One with God is a majority."

We've all read sentences like this.

Some of us have even believed them. But have we practically and in our own every-day existence ever made them work, ever demonstrated them? What' s the good of God if He won't help us to meet the rent, to get a job, to be happy — if He isn't available every moment of the day to us?

The great power which created the *I am* within you is always available. He will take care of the upkeep.

Instead of taking yourself at the valu-ation of Professor Poofinfoos, you must take yourself at God's valuation.

If I had stopped to listen to all the unpleasant predictions that Poofinfoos has made to me, and particularly to his insinuations and threats, I doubt if I would be here today. As it was, he talked me into more sickness and discord and trouble and problems than I care to think about. Never did I start anything in my professional life that he didn't in some way try to stop or wreck. He seemed always to be trying to prevent me from accomplishing my purpose. He sneaked into my business, he even sneaked into my home with his suggestions of discord and confusion.

At least he did until I got sick and tired of it, and then I decided I was going to take charge of my own life and not let Madame Flitmajigger and Professor Poofinfoos dominate it any longer. So out they went! Booted out! The pair of them. Now I am trying to be watchful enough to see that they don't slip back through the door of my thinking and start something else unpleasant. I find it much safer to keep them out than to let them get inside and try later to put them out.

Back of the glamour that motion pictures have thrown around me, I am just an average, hopeful, prayerful woman. I have had many griefs and many trials in my life. I started — as we all seem to start — full of fear, full of distresses, worrying and fretting, carrying burdens that didn't belong to me, thinking I was responsible for running everything for everybody. I had to learn to stop trying to be Atlas and carrying the world on my shoulders, to stop wearing the Captain's cap and let God do the navigating.

Please know that what I have said here is said in all humility and because I have proved it.

I haven't solved all my problems as yet, but I shall; for I have learned that as I take care of my thinking, my thinking takes care of me in every little detail of my life.

Isn't it worth trying?

AFTERWORD

In 1934, silent film actress Mary Pickford published a booklet entitled *Why Not Try God?* From its title, one would be inclined to catalogue it under "spiritual guidance" or "advice literature," and if one was to leaf through its pages one would find it offers both a vision on spirituality as well as practical, friendly advise on life and living. During the teens and twenties Mary Pickford had known her biggest successes as a silent film performer. Nicknamed, "America's Sweetheart," she had been praised for her comic and sympathetic turns in sentimental films for family audiences, and had been known for her celebrity marriage as well as for her business sense and acquired fortune. How does a book with a title like, *Why Not Try God?* fit in with the star's career and personality?

First of all, it is important to remember that the book was published *after*

Pickford's active screen career, at a time when her professional and private life were in serious turmoil as she was trying to reroute her career and was struggling to save her marriage to Douglas Fairbanks. It is therefore not unreasonable to assume that, in part, the booklet was written therapeutically, as an answer to Pickford's own doubts and questions. Second, Pickford had tried her hand at writing before and had already been a provider of what one could call a form of testimonial advice (often bordering on lay-therapeutics) in articles, columns or interviews. *Why Not Try God?* was not a first and so it might prove enlightening to look at her earlier writings.

Pickford had tried her hand at different types of texts in the past. When she first appeared on the silent screen in the early 1910s, she had now and again written her own screenplays to create interesting parts for herself. Later, when fame and stardom came she gladly contributed articles for fan magazines. Between 1915 and 1917, Pickford even authored a syndicated advice column called *Daily Talks with Mary Pickford* in which she mused on a variety of subjects such as life, love, the film industry, frugality, work and its rewards, women's rights, old-fashioned domestic ideals, beauty secrets and answered questions from her fans. It would seem that these columns tapped into a tradition of conduct manuals or prescriptive literature, which had been popular in the United States since the nineteenth century. These conduct manuals addressed their readers in a familiar and friendly but also hortatory fashion and presented models on how to be. The authors of these books typically assumed a position of expertise and moral superiority and they had been principally educators, ministers, and mothers. However, the twentieth century saw movie stars like Pickford (but also Douglas Fairbanks, Colleen Moore, and Rudolph Valentino) take an interest in the genre and audiences generally accepted the life lessons these stars had to teach them. We could say that the publication of *Why Not Try*

God? in 1934 saw Pickford in fact *return* to a part she had played in the most successful days of her career: that of role model and confidante.

Most of Mary's texts were ghostwritten but Pickford's voice and personality can be discerned from the texts regardless of who the ghostwriter actually was. Partly this can be explained by the fact that Pickford was usually very close to the writers who ghosted for her. One of them was her good friend and frequent scenario writer, Frances Marion. Another good friend, Adela Rogers St. Johns, known as a sharp celebrity columnist but also a sensitive writer who shared Pickford's religious views, was engaged to write *Why Not Try God?* (and later *My Rendezvous with Life*) in the thirties. Writers like Marion and Rogers St. Johns knew exactly what Pickford "sounded" like, and Pickford's voice is remarkably consistent in all her (ghosted) writings. Of course, Pickford had always had a clear sense of what her morals and ideals amounted to, and how she wanted these embodied in her public persona. In addition, she was extremely prudent in safeguarding the quality of every product associated with her name and person, and she carefully pondered over each word that was printed in her name.

Why Not Try God? is presented as the sincere, intimate record of Pickford's own struggle to come to a fulfilling understanding of God. It is written in the same vein as her advice columns of the past, mixing anecdote, rhetorical questions, and metaphorical figures to dramatize a point. It celebrates the power of thought and positive thinking and connects with the basic tenets of Christian Science. According to a 1934 portrait of the actress in the *New York Times*, Pickford added her own staunch determination, her optimism containing a "quality of fierceness" to Mary Baker Eddy's creed. Some critics detected (unfavorably) a Pollyanna-esque philosophy in Pickford's unfailing optimism, but from Pickford's perspective the *Pollyanna* comparison must have been judged much more favorably: just as the film adaptation of *Pollyanna* in 1920 had once brought her financial success, the Pollyanna-vision that can be discerned in *Why Not Try God?* had now brought her spiritual peace as well. And the book in which she professed these beliefs would become, providentially, another bestseller.

Even though the many readers that made the book a bestseller at its first publication must have bought the book because of Pickford's enduring fame, the retired actress closes her book by stressing how mainstream her convictions really are, how "average" she really is. She notes humbly: "Back of the glamour that motion pictures have thrown around me, I am just an average, hopeful, prayerful woman." A star may have written the book but the story it tells is that of an "average" woman looking for answers and sharing them with the world.

ANKE BROUWERS
ANTWERP, 2013

ABOUT THE
AFTERWARD AUTHOR

Dr. Anke Brouwers teaches film history and film theory courses at the University of Antwerp and Hogeschool Gent (Kask – School of Arts). She has written a PhD on sentimentalism in the films of Mary Pickford and Frances Marion.

She has published in Quarterly Review of Film and Video, Film International and has contributed to edited collections (e.g. Slapstick Comedy, 2009, Melodrama, 2012) and conference proceedings. Research interests include cinematic narration, film and emotion, children's cinema, silent cinema and intermediality

ABOUT THE AUTHOR

Film pioneer, businesswoman, author and philanthropist Mary Pickford (1892-1979), frequently called "America's Sweetheart," was for at least twenty years of the last century the most famous woman in the world. Though best known as a star and producer of motion pictures during the silent film era, her ideas have had a profound influence on popular culture up to today.

Made in United States
Orlando, FL
10 February 2024

43529319R00029